LEATHER CRAFT FOR TODAY

By
Dorothee KOECHLIN-SCHWARTZ-BIZEMONT

DRAKE PUBLISHERS INC.   NEW YORK

ISBN 0-87749-467-3
LCCC N 73-3717
Published in 1973 by
Drake Publishers Inc
381 Park Avenue South
New York, N.Y. 10016

The Bible tells us that " When Adam and Eve noticed that they were naked, they covered themselves with fig leaves"... It certainly looked prettier and more suitable to the Mediterranean climate of a terrestrial paradise!

Unfortunately, it appears that things then changed because most prehistoric paintings and engravings ignored the fig-leaf dress and infer that our ancestors took to wearing animal hides: furs, leather and all kinds of skins.

The wearing of leather probably goes back to the very distant past, not only for clothing but also for a great number of indispensable objects — shoes, bags, containers (in particular, goatskin bottles containing water and liquids), tents, belts, goatskin bottles containing water and liquids), saddles, harnesses etc.

With country folk, living naturally from their livestock, leather was — and still is — a material of fundamental importance which the competition of vegetable materials has in no way eliminated. (Note for example, the wonderful craftsmanship of desert peoples.) In the great oriental and occidental sedentary civilizations, leather has kept an extremely important place.

A few mournful souls have thought that leather was out dated and that in the years to come it will be replaced entirely by "synthetic" materials which are cheap and which are perfect imitations. But to date the particular qualities of leather — smell, touch, and a whole set of physio-chemical properties which give leather its particular charm — remain quite impossible to reproduce synthetically.

Leather maintains a perfect shape when properly handled, which is not the case with plastics which lose their shape far more quickly. It is tougher and resists infinitely better when put to daily use. A low conductor of heat, it is also far better for your health than all the imitation leathers made from plastic. Just think of a car seat unbearably overheated on a scorchingly hot day.

INTRODUCTION

It is therefore a material from the past and, at the same time, modern on which we're going to work. Naturally, this does not mean becoming a "professional" but simply learning to use leather to the best of one's ability and making "creations" which are both attractive and practical.

5 7/8"

7 1/4"
Poker-work purse (p.88)

EQUIPMENT

WHAT IS MEANT EXACTLY BY "LEATHER" AND "SUEDE":

A few simple definitions first of all:

A skinned animal shed of its fur or hair (pig "bristles" for example) provides **LEATHER.** This is made up of two distinct parts:

1) The **Hair-side** (the outer side which is co-covered with hair)

2) The **Crust** or **Flesh** (inner lining side)

Suede is a crust which is treated in a special way, giving it a certain velvety appearance.

We will not enter into the details of the tanning process here, as they are complicated industrial processes and do not come into the picture for the type of work described in this book.

Let's just say that there exists a **large variety of leather and skins:** cat, dog, buckskin (the real type), crocodile, lizard, whale, seal, ostrich... The ones most commonly used are:

- Calf (called "box-calf")
- Sheep skin
- Goat and kid (called Morocco)
- Pig

Crocodile skin gets such a high price that it is impractical for amateur use. But on the contrary one can find goat, calf and sheep skin relatively cheaply in this country.

5

Common qualities:

● Elasticity:

The skin consists of fine fibers which slide one over the other, especially when wet. Some leathers are more elastic than others and certain parts in the same skin are more elastic than others.

Before beginning work on an object, one must make sure that the piece of leather won't become misshapen (very fine skins being more susceptible in this respect). To prevent this simply pull the skin a little to see if it stretches easily.

● Leather **can be glued** far more successfully than cloth: There are some excellent glues on the market which are so strong that two pieces of leather can't be separated once they have been glued together. They may tear but the glued parts stay stuck together.

● Leather **does not fray:**

This is a further advantage compared to cloth: if you are making clothes you can leave out the hem and, in any case, the overcasting. This rigidity in leather makes the work easier and faster.

Common drawbacks:

● For work on **large surfaces**, the big whole skins are **somewhat expensive** and don't possess the continuity that cloth does. This means one has to assemble a quantity of skins if one wishes to have a big surface.

This inconvenience is compensated by the very low cost of leather remnants. We will discuss this further on.

● The **upkeep** of leather is more difficult than that of cloth or plastic materials. Leather reacts unfavorably to water (except varnished leathers which are produced today). Light-colored suedes are very fragile: the slightest raindrop leaves a mark. Darker colors are obviously more practical; water marks and other stains are less visible.

It is never advisable to wash leather. It should be cleaned either at a specialized dry-cleaners or one may clean the stains oneself with special leather cleaner.

Stains can also be removed, according to their type, with turpentine, trichlorethylene or ether.

WHERE TO FIND LEATHER AND SUEDE

• **At Home**, First of all: On looking through closets you may find on old leather or suede coat, old handbags or different objects which may not have been used for years but now may come in handy: briefcases, map cases, belts, gloves, or cushions for example. Before plastic materials came onto the market a great many common objects were made of leather (toilet and beauty cases, suitcases, chair seat covers, etc.).

• At any **thrift shop** or second-hand store. You can thus buy used coats or jackets that will provide a large sized piece of leather or suede.

• **Craftsmen** who make clothes in leather or skins sell remnants by weight at very low prices from their workshops, and which, in spite of their small size, are perfectly workable. As leather is relatively light a fraction of a pound of leather can provide a pretty good amount at a relatively low cost.

Some workshops re-use all the big pieces and only sell the left-overs. Others sell amongst these left-overs large piece of leather which are big enough to make bags, boleros, wide belts...

One slight drawback: manufacturers produce a majority of clothing in dark shades (black, chestnut, brown, beige...) because they sell better. As for bright colors, they depend upon the whims of fashion.

• **Leather tanners** sell at reduced prices skins that are unsuitable for sale or industrial use, skins that are "faulty" but which are perfectly adaptable for our use.

- Finally **leathercrafts stores or hobby shops** can supply leather remnants upon demand.

- If you have the money to afford one or several whole skins in perfect condition, you must get them through Skin and Leather Merchants and not through Tanners who sell exclusively to wholesalers and manufacturers.

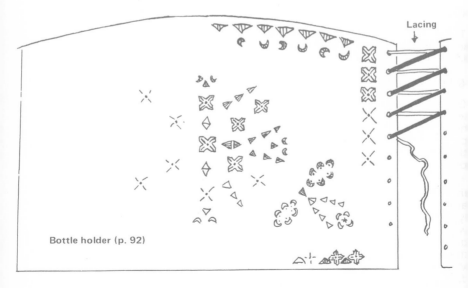

Lacing

Bottle holder (p. 92)

TECHNIQUES

Some information concerning the terms and techniques used

We must point out that not all techniques are given here. We will deal with those techniques which guide our work, deliberately leaving aside those which are typically professional.

GLUED LEATHER:

There are many excellent glues that are found without difficulty at any hardware store or leathercraft shop.

GILDED LEATHER:

Gold (silver, or different colors) is sold in thin leaves which are applied to leather with a heated "gilders iron" or with the end of a poker. This latter procedure is quite easy and the tools are sold on the market at reasonable prices.

"Hot gilding" used a lot in the olden days in France, has gone out of fashion and there are very few gilders left in this country (usually, but not always, they are book binders as well). In other countries on the contrary, and particularly in Italy (especially in Florence), the Maghreb countries, (Morocco, Tunis), the Middle and Near East, (Iran, Afghanistan, India...) the techniques of gilding remain very much alive.

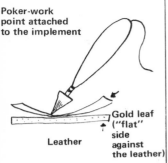

Poker-work point attached to the implement

Gold leaf ("flat" side against the leather)

Leather

Viennese lacing

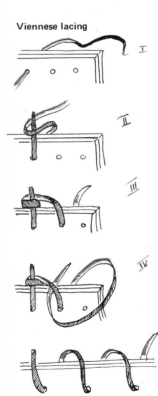

Gilding is done in the following manner: the heated point is applied onto gold leaf placed flat onto the leather (the "flat" side of the gold leaf against the leather and the brilliant side on the surface). You should experiment first to test the right temperature. If too cold, the gold does not "take"; too hot, it melts and produces a mixture of leather and burnt gold.

In other words, gilding is a sort of transfer. Other techniques for gilding exist, which are more refined and which are unnecessary to mention here. They require a serious apprenticeship.

LACED LEATHER

A fairly easy Viennese technique: You do not sew leather in the normal sense but tie it together edge to edge with a strip of kid skin.

With this strip a series of laced knots are threaded through holes pre-pierced in the leather (see drawing).

This strip of kid-skin, measuring from 1 to 2 eighths of an inch wide looks like a thread wound around a reel (1).

If this fails, they can cut them out from a fine, shiny skin (with a ruler and razor blade), but the strips on reels are more even and solid than those made by an amateur.

To thread the strips through the 2 pieces of leather, you must pierce fairly large holes and above all they must be evenly spaced. You can:

● in the same way as professional craftsmen, use a toothed cutting tool to allow for even perforation spacing.

● with a tape measure and pencil, mark in

(1) Sold in artists supply shops and leather craft stores

advance evenly spaced holes and punch them with a paper punch, a pair of scissors or any sharp pointed instrument.

Various lacing techniques are used (see drawing): you can thread a strip into a big needle or simply thread it through the holes to form:

• an overstitch with two pieces of leather.

All these combinations are feasible and simply require a little imagination.

LEATHER MOSAICS:

This consists of a juxtaposition of leathers of different qualities and colors. The traditional skilled technique can be simplified. We will simply make leather mosaics by gluing different pre-cut pieces and superimposing them.

TOOLED LEATHER

Decoration is carried out with the aid of "chisels" (iron points in which the underside is engraved like a stamp or seal). There are several different types: star shaped, flower-shaped, triangular, and those covered with small spikes etc. The chisel is applied to the dampened leather and is struck with a wooden mallet or hammer.

POKER-WORK LEATHER

With the aid of the pointed end of a poker heated over a small stove, the leather is burned in small light touches (do not overheat). Suede can also be Poker-worked and the effect is more refined.

DYED LEATHER:

You can have fun at home dying light-colored leather, with very favorable results. Some shops supplying artist's materials sell excellent leather

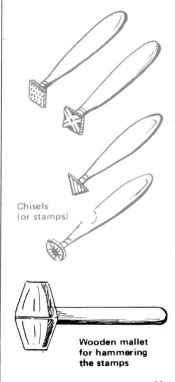

Chisels
(or stamps)

Wooden mallet
for hammering
the stamps

dyes. At home Mercurochrome for vermillion and methylene blue can also be used.

First of all we will work upon industrially dyed leather, keeping home-made dyes for certain colors to match our selected colors when we are no longer able to obtain them.

LEATHER AND SUEDE CLOTHES: CUTTING OUT AND MAKING UP:

Patterns are used in the same way as patterns for cloth.

Cut leather and suede with tailors scissors remembering to cut downwards always (the hair starts from the head and "works down" toward the tail), therefore following the line of the hair.

Never place side-by-side two pieces of suede where the hair grows in opposite directions. It is easily noticeable!

The cut clothes are assembled by stitching on the machine. Please note, small family sewing machines are not strong enough for most leathers and suedes which are too thick. If you try it you might break the needle or even the machine. Only exceptionally fine leathers (sheered sheepskin, for example) can be stitched with our ordinary sewing machines.

To hand stitch you should not use a needle with a rounded body as used for saddle-stitching, but a **grooved triangular-shaped needle**, with a strong pointed end which can be found at a fabric or notions store. Don't try to use an ordinary sewing needle, the result is discouraging — pricked fingers, broken needles...

A very tough thread (linen thread for buttons for example) is necessary. Hems may be glued. They are not indispensable: many clothes have fringed hems, Western style. It is advisable to mark out with a pencil (or ball-point pen) before cutting to prevent the scissors from going off the mark. They can also be cut **out with a razor blade along a ruler's edge (for the rectilinear edges).**

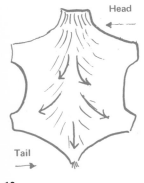

Head

Tail

"Exotic" techniques

EMBROIDERED LEATHER AND SUEDE:

Embroidered leather still exists in North Africa, in the Middle East, Afghanistan, Pakistan, India, Muslim Soviet Asia.

The "Putchinsta" fashion from Afghanistan, brought back into fashion by the hippies, reveals the beauty of the fur coat lined on the exterior with silk embroidered suede from Afghanistan. The technique is one of the simplest — a grooved triangular shaped needle, silk thread, a thimble — no different from our own normal methods of embroidering, if only in the origins of the motifs: Persian flowers, fruits and leaves in arabesques. Certain towns in Maghreb specialize in the embroidery of Turkish slippers, belts (Fez, Marrakech, Tunisian craftsmanship etc.), enlivened according to whim with beads and tiny mirrors.

LEATHER AND COPPER: DIFFERENT COVERS FROM THE BY-GONE "CORDOVANS":

For a long time the town of Cordova in Spain was the unrivalled capital of the leather industry and in America its memory lives on through the name "Cordovan leather". Amongst the most note-worthy products of this city were objects covered in leather, metal plating and brass nails; chair seats and above all chests which at that period served as suitcases, trunks, and sometimes as hanging cupboards.

The tradition of leather seats has been carried on into our era. The traditional chest has flowered for many years in Spain, and some beautiful "Pirate chests" can be found at antique dealers and in old houses.

During the "Conquest" the Moslem craftsmen, thrown out of Spain, found refuge in Fez in Morocco, where they continued the art of

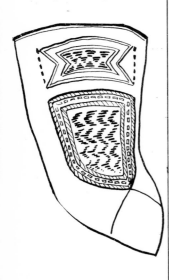

**Haoussa boot
(Southern Sahara,
Niger and Nigeria)**

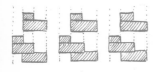

Example
of woven
leather strips

leather work. The "Moroccan" work stands as a witness to the renown of this craftsmanship since the end of the Middle Ages.

Even today the tourist may buy, not only in Fez but also in Algeria and Tunis, these chests, which are made according to ancient methods right before his eyes. And not only chests, but belts, handbags and satchels, straps with shiny bright nails, rivets, brass plaques and even money on a leather background.

BRAIDED LEATHER:

The Saharan peoples braided leather by using either strips of their own or those combined with threads and woolen pom-poms, or mixed with beads and shells.

All nomadic or semi-nomadic peoples living in the vast desert regions which stretch from the Atlantic to India and China, utilize and work leather as an essential raw material. For centuries it was easier to acquire a sheep skin than a length of material, because the aridness of the Steppes and the poverty of the oasis prevented the cultivation of textile plantations (such as flax, hemp, cotton). This situation has greatly changed, especially in Soviet Asia.

An interesting technique consists of weaving different colored leathers within a larger piece so as to create a geometric design comparable to those of woven materials (see drawing). As we have seen, the Touaregs and various other ethnic groups from the Southern Sahara decorate shoes and bags this way.

Other ideas...

Such rich matter lends itself to a host of new ways and means of working leather and the list of techniques which we have mentioned is far from being exhausted.

Braided leather can, for example, be blended with pebbles found on the beach (which are stuck on).

Very thick leathers can be painted with transparent oil paint.

In fact, anything which your imagination suggests can be invented.

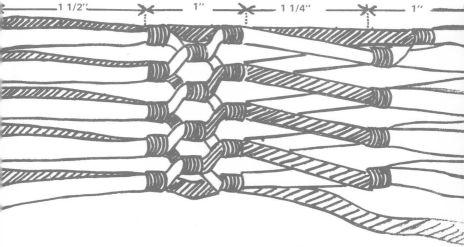

Detail of the bag shown on page 45

METHODS

TOOLS

For every chapter we will give you in two lists the necessary tools:

• Indispensable technical tools

• The particular tools necessary for each method.

Where to find these tools?

In most cases they are simple and fairly easy to manipulate. It will suffice to use the tools found in any well equipped household, plus a few small purchases from the hardware store.

When a tool is hard to find on the market, it should be bought at any big hardware store or in an artist's supply or leather craft shop.

Finally, the last category of tools can be obtained from one or more manufacturers.

For your reference the name of each implement or tools is followed by one or several asterisks:

* At any clothing stores, hardware stores...

** Big hardware or department stores, book shops selling educational material, shops selling artist's materials

*** Manufacturing firms specializing in the supply of tools for diverse types of craftsmanship.

In general the prices for these tools are not very high. The articles selected in this book have been chosen with an eye to their low cost.

The only exceptions are the necessary equipment for gilding and Poker-work.

COLLAGES

Necessary equipment

- Leather glue.
- Paper Punch.
- Stapler.
- Tape measure and set-square.
- Ball-point pen or chalk.
- Large pointed trimming scissors.
- Razor blade.
- Cardboard for backing the pictures.

Technical characteristics

- Adults may have the same fun as very young children (from 3-4 years of age) in making a collage.
- The cost is very low because all sorts of leather remnants can be utilized, even the very smallest.
- Certain glues leave smudges, which can usually be removed quite easily with turpentine — not for every type of glue however.

GLUED NAPKIN RING

See photo on page 25. Time required: 2 hours.

Special material

See list at the beginning of chapter

• A rectangular piece of leather or suede measuring 2 1/2" x approximately 7 1/2" (exact measurements don't matter).

• A snap fastener (have this fixed by a shoemaker if you don't wish to go to the expense of buying a special punch). **

• Brightly colored leather remnants.

Method

• Attach the snap fastener. The pointed extremity of the leather should cover the square extremity, don't make a mistake in fixing the two parts of the snap fastener the wrong way on.

• Select light colored remnants for a darker background (here pink, orange, grey, on an ultra-marine background).

• With scissors, cut out the designs reproduced in the drawing. Mark guiding points with a ball-point pen and glue at the chosen points.

• The tiny circles should be cut from brightly colored leather with the help of a punch. Naturally these designs can be varied from the more elementary to the most refined.

TAPESTRY IN GLUED LEATHER AND MIRRORS

See list at the beginning of the chapter. *

Special material

See list at the beginning of the chapter.

• Fairly large leather or suede remnants of the same color for the background (here "rust" suede).

• Small leather remnants of different colors, thickness and quality (here glossy white, black, beige, steel grey, grey blue, bright pink suede and leather).

• An old mirror with a fine glass.

• A piece of cardboard measuring 12 1/2" x 16".

• Glossy ultra-marine cotton thread, triangular needle and thimble.

Specifications

• The type of work small children love. You can choose a simple design or let their imagination flow.

Method

The Background:

Onto the cardboard glue large pieces of leather of the same color (here, "rust" suede).

It is better to have a large piece of leather the same size as the cardboard. If not, place the remnants side by side and cut off the pieces overlapping the edges of the cardboard.

Flowers and Leaves:

Draw each design on paper with a ball-point pen. Then trace them several times onto the reverse side of the pieces of leather or suede.

Note that certain designs are used on the "leather side" and others on the "suede side". The black leaves are used on the "leather side".

Very small circles are made with the paper punch. You can mix these designs and play around with their shapes. Their composition can result in many varied patterns. The one chosen here can be simplified or complicated.

Mirrors:

Break up an old mirror with a hammer to get pieces of required size. You will never succeed in creating round mirrors this way, nor heart-shaped mirrors nor square ones, but more likely elongated pieces which can be shaped by framing them with leather.

Embroidery of Round Mirror Flowers:

Button-hole stitch the frame for each mirror with the glossy ultra-marine cotton (the inner edge of the smallest circle on the sketch).

Round flowers

Fragment of mirror

Embroider the frame of the mirror

Glue the mirror on the background circle

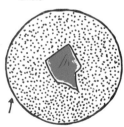

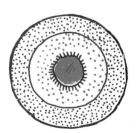

Glue the embroidered frame onto the background circle

19

This results in a gradual range of colors starting from the center working outwards: ultramarine blue, grey blue, light grey mirrors. This selectivity can be done away with for very young children.

Glue the Design:

A few simple rules:

• Before gluing them, spread out on the background all the designs to see if anything has been forgotten, and to check whether the design is satisfactory and to your taste.

• For the round flowers, place the mirror on a big steel blue circle and cover with an embroidered steel blue circle. The same procedure is used for the other designs in which a mirror is used: this is placed between its 2 frames.

• Always mark out with a ball-point pen and a ruler. Draw the outlines of the different designs so as to place them in exactly the same spot after having covered them with glue.

• Glue is used like any ordinary glue. Apply glue to one side only.

Framing the Design:

Here we have cut out long narrow bands (¹/₄") to underline the frame and we have bordered the whole thing with black tape (if desired, you can leave it this way).

Suggestions

Leather glue adheres very well and this allows you to stretch your imagination to other objects: belts, bags, cushions, lamp shades, table cloths (protected by glass), etc.

Children's bedrooms can be decorated in this way (doors, cupboards, beds, chair seats, chests, clothes hangers etc). Children will love it because they like the soft touch of leather.

Give children ready cut-out pieces of leather and they will enjoy imagining different ways of gluing them onto cardboard (or material covered cardboard).

Central heart 1

Fragment of mirror

1st mirror frame (black heart cut-out)

2nd mirror frame

Glue onto the 3rd larger frame

Glue the mirror onto the 2nd frame and the black cut-out heart on top

21

CAT, IN THE "DOUANIER ROUSSEAU" STYLE

See photo on page 31. Time required: 1 day.

Necessary equipment

See list at the beginning of the chapter.*

• A square piece of cardboard measuring 21 3/4" x 16 1/4".

• A piece of black material (felt, imitation felt, thick woolen cloth) measuring 23" x 16 3/4".

• Leather remnants in brown, beige, chestnut, black, white. 2 small pieces of black leather.

Method

Prepare the Background:

Stretch the black material onto cardboard and fasten behind with a stapler. Glue if the staples don't hold.

Pattern of the Cat:

Taking our ideas from the sketches opposite, draw up a pattern of a cat according to the required size (use tracing paper if you don't know how to draw).

From the sketch draw up the different parts which make up the body and head of the animal. If you are hesitant, number the different parts of the sketch and apply them to the corresponding pattern.

Putting the Pattern on the Leather:

No particular difficulty. Place the parts of the pattern on the leather remnants, trace the outline with a pencil or ball-point pen and cut out to the design.

Sticking on the Different Parts:

"Assemble" the cat before gluing it, laying out correctly each part, one on the other, so as to make any necessary adjustments.

Begin by gluing the under pieces, and then the smaller details. If need be, mark the points before final gluing.

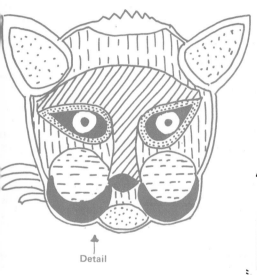

↑
Detail

The different parts of the cat's head

General outline of the cat

16 1/4"

9 3/4"

Necessary equipment

- Pointed scissors.
- Tape measure, ball-point pen.
- Glossy linen thread and triangular-shape needle. *
- A box of steel eyelets (one eighth of a inch in diameter). **
- A box of brass eyelets (one eighth of a inch in diameter). **
- An eyelet punch to fix them. **

- Beads: 1 box of steel beads or a few boxe of brightly colored beads to contrast with th leather.
- A box of press-studs. **

- Steel and brass rings in different sizes (thre eighths of an inch and seven eighths of an inc wide). *

- Remains of brightly colored balls of wool.

- Several brass and steel "S's" in differer sizes. The larger "S's" are quite hard to com by. **
- A box of gilt fasteners.
- Leather glue.
- An ordinary pair of pincers, or even bette a pincer known as a rosary tweezers. Eyebro tweezers can also come in handy. **
- A reel of brass thread.
- Ordinary tweezers.

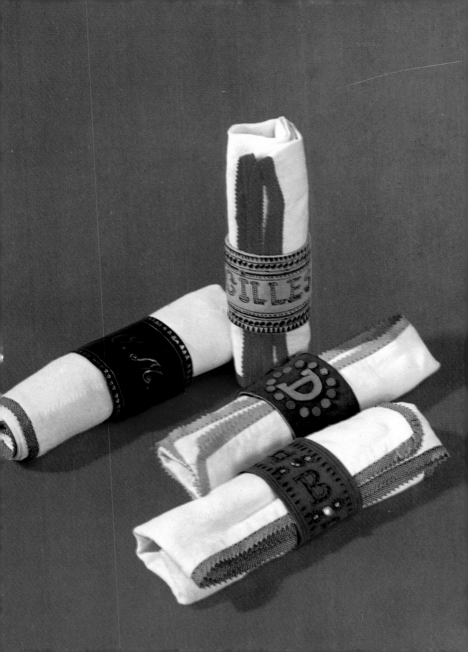

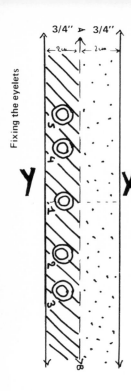

3/4'' ⊁ 3/4''

Y   X

Characteristics of the leather
Lucky dip

• The cost varies: Leather is mixed with brass or chrome steel accessories which enhance it but which end up by raising the cost of the object (not necessarily excessively).

• Some accessories are easy to find at the hardware store, others are hard to find: for example, one can find small chrome "S's" anywhere but the bigger brass "S's" are difficult to come by.

• These accessories are easy to manipulate. The eyelet pincers are fun and simple to use; the fasteners, easy to fix, give attractive result, beads lend themselves to a wide range of uses, etc.

DOG COLLAR

See photo on page 67. Time required: 4 hours.

Necessary equipment

Sewing materials. *

• A leather remnant to make a square measuring 21 3/4'' x 1 1/2'' (here purple suede).

• 6 silver colored beads. **

• 5 silver colored eyelets and an eyelet pincer.

Specifications

It is the easiest in the book and will thrill little girls.

If you do not have any eyelets, they can be replaced by beads or tiny leather "circles" stuck on here and there.

Method

• Cut a long strip out of the leather or suede remnant measuring 21 3/4''.

• With the ruler and ball-point pen, trace a

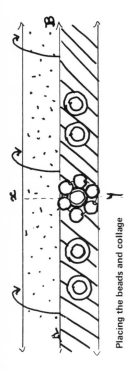

Part to be folded and glued behind

Placing the beads and collage

line AB which divides it lengthwise in half. Mark a guiding point XY in the center of the band of leather.

• In the interior of the band mark 5 points where the eyelets will be attached. One, placed right in the center of XY of the band is the center of the bead design.

• Attach the eyelets (see drawing).

• Thread the 6 beads onto strong linen thread and knot the two ends together (see detailed explanation on page 41). Thus you have a bead crown.

• Sew the bead crown around the central eyelet.

• Fold back the top part of the band along the line AB and glue it behind the underside. Even off with scissors. If the leather is thin, the necklace is tied around the neck with a knot (like a ribbon). If the leather is thicker, fasten it with a press-stud or fix some eyelets into which one can knot a very thin strip of material in a matching color.

Suggestions

Rings, bracelets, belts, hair bands, etc.

SUEDE BELT

See photo on page 67. Time required: 4 hours.

Special equipment

• Fairly thin suede remnants (here, rust colored).

• 6 "gilt" brass rings — 3/4" in diameter. **

• A big brass "S", corresponding to the size of the rings.**

• 20 small brass eyelets. **

Specifications

• Select fine suede which can be handled like

material (folds in the rings) and which is easy to work on. Small remnants may be used.

• If you possess an eyelet pincer, it is extremely easy. If not, ask a shoemaker to attach them.

Method

• Cut out a series of squares, either similar or dissimilar but you must have at least 2 lots of 2 which are identical. Here there are 5 suede squares: 4 big (8 3/4" x 1 1/2"), and one small 6 x 1/2".

Everything obviously depends upon the remnants one possesses: if you have very small remnants you can increase the number of suede squares, but consequently, the number of rings and eyelets, but you must always make sure that the pieces are symmetrical. Moreover, the height must always be the same, whatever the length of the pieces.

• Take the waist measurement of the person who will wear the belt (here 3 1/4").

• Lay out the pieces on a table next to a tape measure or a piece of string the same length as the waist measurement. Pay attention to the symmetry of the pieces, for example: A-B-C-B'-A' (C being the piece of a different size which is placed in the middle, A and A' being of the same length, B and B' also).

• Each strip of suede is slipped through a brass ring and folded back thus losing a little of its length (here, we have folded back 1 1/2" at each end). You can fold back either more or less: it must be done regularly and when completed must correspond with the desired waist size.

• The suede passed through the ring is attached with two eyelets. As the suede is fine, it makes supple pleats when passed through the ring. Each ring joins together two pieces of suede.

• A ring at each end of the belt is left floating. Attach to one of the two brass "S's" which

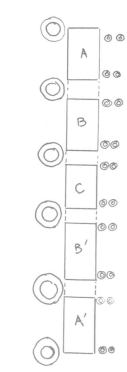

Fixing the ring

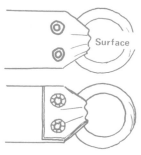

Reverse

fasten the belt (tighten it with an ordinary pincer).

Other pieces of the same sized suede can be glued on the inner side to reinforce the belt.

HIPPIE BRACELET

See photo on page 67. Time required: 2 to 3 hours.

Necessary equipment

Sewing materials *.

● A piece of fine suede 3 3/8'' x 8'' and a few remnants of the same color (here violet).

● 8 steel beads 1/4'' in diameter.

● 6 steel eyelets 1/2'' in diameter or 3 press-studs.

● 3 steel "S's" if eyelets are used.

Specifications

● Can be made by young children in a variety of ways. If they cannot sew the beads evenly, they can stitch on small pre-cut circles.

Method

● With a tape measure and ball-point pen make a paper "pattern". Place the pattern onto the piece of leather and cut out very carefully.
If an error is made while cutting, it is not too serious: just stick a piece of leather under-neath and the cut is thus invisible.

● Sew on the beads having first of all marked out their correct places.

● Attach the 6 eyelets (in our model). If the leather used is really very thin, it can be rein-forced by gluing a strip of suede onto the re-verse side to the eyelet which will then take on the two thicknesses.

● Attach the « S » with ordinary pincers. Leave one extremity more widely open to hook on the facing eyelet.

"S" fastener

30

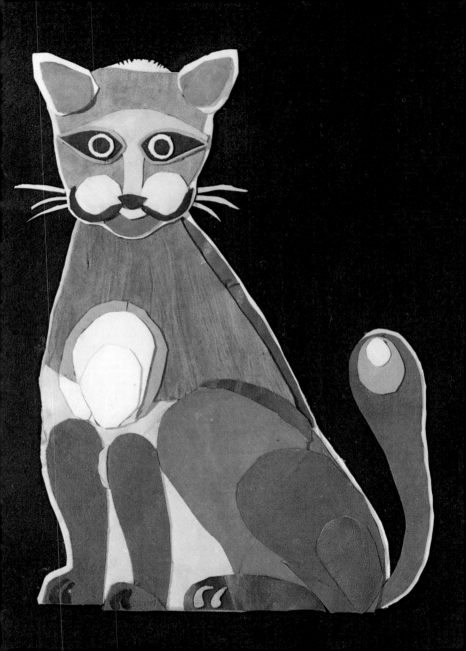

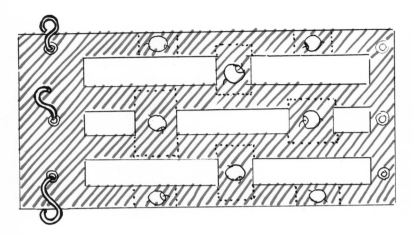

Grouping the strips

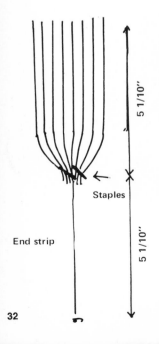

5 1/10"

← Staples

End strip

5 1/10"

• If you have press-stud pincers, you can also fix studs here and there on the bracelet.

• To make certain that the whole is really strong, small pieces of suede can be glued on the reverse side of the bracelet where the beads have been sewn (spot indicated by dots in the sketch).

NECKLACE TO MATCH THE BRACELET

See photo on page 43. Time required: 5 hours.

Special equipment

Sewing materials *

• Leather or suede remnants (here purple).

• Remains of orange, red and bright pink balls of wool.

- A packet of beads (62) in shining steel (the same as for the bracelet).

- A small steel "S".

- 12 small steel rings, 3/8" in diameter.

Method

Preparing the leather strips:

5 times 8 leather strips (or fine suede) plus 2 are needed: a total or 42 strips measuring 5 1/2" length.

If you are lucky enough to have large leather remnants one can prepare 8 strips measuring 19 3/8" (plus 2 strips measuring 5 1/2".
To cut the strips straight, draw a line with a ball-point pen and ruler.

Woolen Beads:

- Take 9 bits of leather strips (either 9 bits of leather strips measuring 5 1/2", or one of the ends of the 8 big strips of 19 3/8" = 1 strip of 5 1/2"). Attach the lot together with one or two staples (this provides a firm hold to work on).

- Leave one strip on one side (the 5 1/2" one if the 8 others are very long). Take the 8 other strips and wrap them around with pink wool.

- When one has a good sized woolen bead (approx. 1" in diameter), and with the help of a needle pass the piece of wool through the head to stop the whole from unwinding.

- String over the whole 2 small rings which will hold the woollen beads into place and liven it up. The rings must not "float".

Threading the Beads:

Thread a bead onto each strip of leather and let it slip without fixing it in any way.

Continuation:

- Still using the staples, fix the 2 floating ends of the 8 strips with the end of 8 fresh strips.

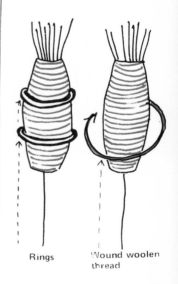

Rings   Wound woolen thread

Begin another thick woolen bead in a different color (orange, pink or red in equal cadence).

● If you have 8 strips measuring 19 3/8", staple them together at interval of 5 1/2" from the first staple (in other words, in the middle of the preceding bead) and make a woolen ball above the staple as above.

● Repeat the threading of the beads etc. To finish, staple the last 8 ends of the strip plus one, and make a bead like the preceding ones.

Leather or Suede Pom-Poms:

● Cut out a small leather or suede square (preferably suede for an ornament), each side measuring 2 3/8". Cut deep fringes into practically the whole surface (leaving a space of 3/4" at the top).

● Wind the fringed square around the last floating strip just underneath the woollen ball. Glue the inner wound surface (leather side of the Pom-pom is on the suede side).

The Pendant Design:

It is made up of 2 triangles (sides measuring 2 3/8") sewn together, which fasten the necklace.

● Take a needle, linen thread, and join the 2 triangles by sewing between them the 2 leather strips which end the necklace and extend beyond the Pom-poms (these should end at the very edges of the triangles).

● Thread a bead on both sides and at each point (11 + 11 beads).

● On the lower point of the triangle, sew on a tongue of leather (or a piece of a leather strip) which forms a knot. This knot holds a small steel chrome "S".

The Finishing Touch:

It consists of 3 colored woolen tassels to match the beads on the necklace: red, bright pink in the middle, orange.

The tassel is made by winding wool around an object (ruler, or evenly pleated paper, or any object with a width of about 1 3/8"). Hold the

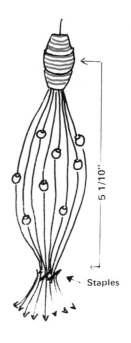

5 1/10"

Staples

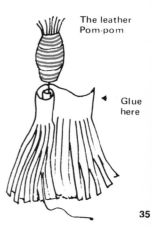

The leather Pom-pom

Glue here

35

strands very tightly at one end and cut the other end.

Thread the 3 Pom-poms onto the "S", which can be closed with a pincer (or with one's fingers if the metal is soft enough).

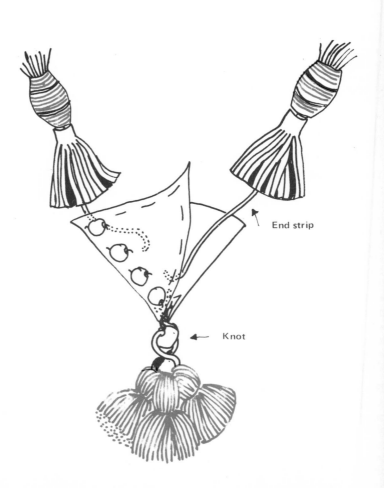

End strip

Knot

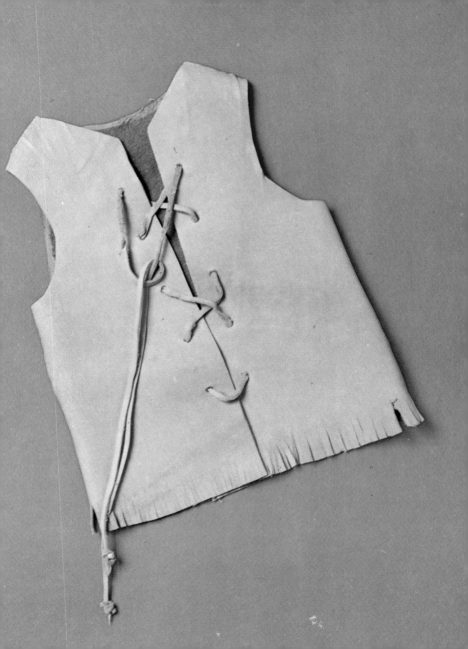

BEADED AND STUDDED BELT

See photo on page 66. Time required: 8 hours.

Necessary equipment

Sewing materials *

- Leather remnants (here, grey).
- 2 boxes of small brass gilt fasteners.
- Assortment of colored beads (here red, orange, bright yellow).
- 2 small gilt belt buckles.

Method

- Decide upon the width desired for the belt. Here it is large: 3 5/8''.

- As from this size, trace the pattern onto paper: a band 3 5/8'' wide and 7 3/4'' to 11 3/4'' in inlength as required.

- Place the paper pattern on the leather remnants. It is not necessary to have large remnants. Whenever a remnant can be used even for a very small part of the belt, use it. Don't forget to mark the out line with a ball-point pen on the reverse of the chosen side for the right place. (Here we have put the "suede" side as the visible side, and the "leather" side as being the reverse.)

- When enough leather remnants have been cut out, each measuring 3 6/10'' width (on different lengths), assemble them on the table by placing them flat. Please bear in mind the following two facts:

The symmetry of the pieces is from the middle of the belt (i.e., the middle of the back). To assemble each piece, 3/4'' is needed, which shortens the total length (as for dress-making, cut the material, bearing in mind the number of inches to be added for the hem).

- Select a length corresponding to the waist measurement of the person who will wear the belt (use an old belt as a guide). Here we have

Top

Lay-out of the belt on a table

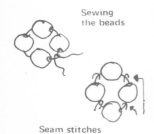

Sewing
the beads

Seam stitches

Grouping the pieces
of leather

Surface

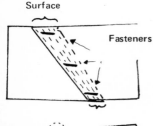

Fasteners

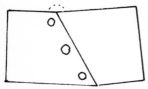

Reverse

taken 30 3/4'' taken the top side and 36 3/10''
for the bottom side.

The two lengths vary because a wide belt must
be molded to the shape of the body. It is nar-
rower around the waist and widens over the
hips. Consequently, when the pieces are laid
out and assembled on the table, don't line
them up squarely but rather in a crescent
shape (see drawing).

Join the pieces of leather with fasteners.

These fasteners are obviously used to group
together the different parts of the belt, but they
further serve for decorative "studding".

• Take 2 pieces of leather and overlap for a
width of 3/4''. This time mark with a ball-point
pen the exact place for the fasteners.

• Pierce the elongated holes lengthened with
the point of a pair of scissors. But pay attention, the slit must be parallel with the edges
of the belt (i.e., horizontal).

• Introduce the fastener into the slit then separate the 2 brass ends from the back. To
separate them completely, you can push downwards with a pair of pincers.

• If a part of the fastener overlaps the edge of
the belt, fold it back or cut it off.

Here we have used regular spacing for the
fasteners: 3 layers one on top of the other (2
along the edges, one in the middle). The fasteners on the edge are spaced at intervals of
about 1 3/8''.

In between the intervening "seams", in other
words in between the pieces of leather, we
have added more fasteners. These are purely
decorative.

Beads:

The following technique is the best:

• First of all, group together and separate the
beads by their color (regardless as tho whether
the designs are round or diamond shaped).
For example, group together 4 yellow, red or
orange beads in the middle; thread them and
tie with a knot.

• Next, place this bead "crown" onto the leather and sew each space between the beads, shaping the beaded crown according to the drawing indicated.

Fixing the Belt Buckles:

• Cut 2 small tongues of the same size as the buckles and thread them as you would any belt buckle — either onto the middle rod, or on one of the edges. Attach the 2 extremities of the tongue onto the belt with the help of a fastener.

Opposite the buckles, place 2 other tongues punched with the appropriate holes to allow fastening.

Finishing Touches:

• The reverse side of the belt is unattractive; the seams and tongue fasteners are visible. To give a smooth uniform look, with leather glue, glue on pieces of suede cut out to the same dimensions (side by side).

• With a rulèr and a pair of scissors trim the belt. As it is made of many pieces, the effect is not always perfectly uniform. On the inner side of the belt mark a straight line (very slightly rounded as the belt is slightly crescent shaped) and cut off whatever overlaps.

SMALL DECORATED BELT

See photo on page 67. Time required: 4 hours.

Special equipment

• A length of fairly thick leather (here 1/10''). This should be very long (here, 38 1/2'') and 3/4'' wide - plus a small piece of the same leather measuring 2 1/2'' x 2 1/2''.

• A pair of eyelet pincers with 30 assorted eyelets (here small eyelets 3/10'' in diameter). **

• 20 big fasteners.

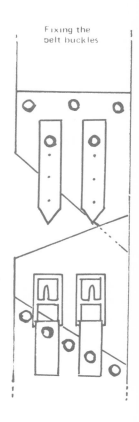

Fixing the belt buckles

41

Eyelet punch

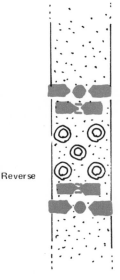

Reverse

• A belt buckle corresponding to the width of the strip of leather.

Naturally, eyelets and buckle must be of the same color: brass or steel.

Specifications

• This necessitates certain tools (a pair of eyelet pincers) and a large strip of leather. Unless you re-shape an old belt, remnants of sufficient quality and thickness sold by craftsmen are hard to find.

• Another problem: the difficulty in hand-cutting thick leather neatly... As an alternative, take 2 or 3 strips of fine leather (easier to cut cleanly) which can then be glued together.

• It cannot be made by young children because a certain muscular effort is needed to pierce the thickness of the leather and to fix in the eyelets.

A punch, regularly perforated, can be used: this is preferable but not absolutely necessary and in any case requires muscular effort if the leather is thick.

Method

• Mark out the guiding points. Here we have 5 lots of eyelets to form 5 central designs. Keep aside 5 eyelets which should be spaced to fasten the belt, and another lot at the other end. Then attach the buckle (leave 3/4'' of the belt bare to keep the buckle in place - see drawing).

Attaching the Eyelets:

• On the place you have pre-marked with the ball-point pen, make a hole either with a punch or with the pointed end of the scissors. The hole should be fairly large to place the eyelet.

• Attach the eyelet with pincers.

Attaching the Fasteners:

• Pierce an elongated hole parallel to the length of the belt and slide in the fastener.

• On the reverse side separate the two bands of the fastener. Flatten them downwards by pushing hard with an ordinary pincer. If the bands overlap, fold them back carefully. On our model the fasteners are placed on the surface and on the reverse side as both ways are decorative. (The fasteners placed on the reverse side have their bands folded around the leather band, as shown in the drawing.)

Fitting on the Buckle:

• After having threaded the leather band through the buckle, fold it back. Attach it with 3 eyelets. Add on a fastener.

• To make the slot, cut out a leather band measuring 2 1/2" to 2 1/2" long and 1/2" wide. Fold over and fasten with an eyelet.

AN ELEGANT HANDBAG

See photo on page 34.

Time required: 3 days.

Special equipment

Sewing materials.

• Five black leather remnants.

• A square of black leather measuring 5 1/8" x 7 3/4".

• A black felt square (or imitation felt or thick material) measuring 8 3/4" x 12 6/10".

• A spool of gilt brass thread.

• Four brass eyelets, in 2/10" in diameter and an eyelet pincer to fix them.

• 2 brass "S's" which can be passed through the eyelet.

• A brass linked chain 35 3/4" long.**

• A black press-stud or zipper measuring 3 1/4".

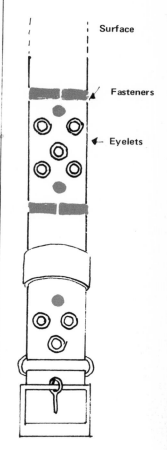

Surface

Fasteners

Eyelets

Method

The Leather Strips:

• Cut out 30 strings of leather measuring 2/10''
x 8 3/4''. Be careful, mark with a ball-point pen
and ruler the lines defining the strips and cut
along these lines. If you don't take this precaution, the strips will turn out very uneven!

• Divide them into 3 groups of 10.

• Divide the first group of 10 strips of leather
in pairs together on a table (i.e. 5 pairs).

• Take the first pair and tie in the following
manner: 1 1/2'' from the end of the strips, wind
a double gilt brass thread measuring 7 3/4''.
Wind — use a pincer if necessary. When this
has been wound round 6 times, cut the brass
thread and tuck the ends under the binding.

• Fix the 4 other pairs of leather strips in the
same way, as shown on the sketch opposite
marked A, B, C, D, E.

• Then attach the strips in between them
threaded through the alternative strips in the
points F, G, H, I. The binding is done with a
strip from each pair. 2 strips float free here
and there.

• Begin the brass binding over again, as many
times as is indicated on the drawing and in
the right order: J, K, L, M, N, etc. For spacing,
see the spaces shown on the drawing on
page 15.

Attaching on the groups of leather strips:

• They are attached onto the little leather
rectangle measuring 5 7/8'' x 7 3/4''. They can
be stapled or sewn.

When the strips are attached, cut their extremities to give them an even, fringed effect.

Attaching the transversal chains:

• Cut the chain into 3 parts with the pincers:
2 measuring 7 1/2'' and one measuring 19 3/4''.

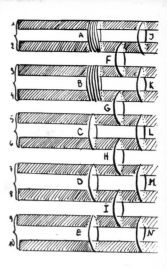

Sketch of the
making-up of
the leather strips

Detail

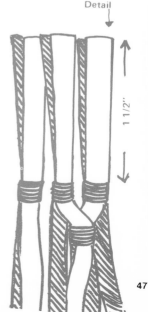

1 1/2''

• Sew the 2 pieces measuring 7 1/2'' onto the leather rectangle between the groups of leather strips (see drawing).

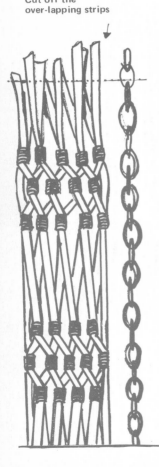

Cut off the over-lapping strips

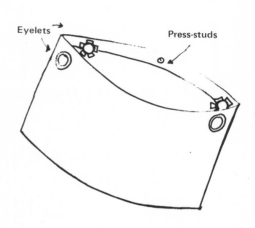

Eyelets →

Press-studs

The Material Bag and its Handle:

• Sew the big square of material (8 3/4'' x 12 1/2'') into a pocket shape.

• Close it with the press-stud or zip fastener.

• Fix an eyelet onto each of the top corners of the bag (see drawing).

• Separate the buckles of each "S" with a pincer. Slip a buckle through the two facing eyelets and other buckle onto a ring of the chain. Shut the "S" buckle.

For use as a handle we have prepared above a piece of chain measuring 16 3/4''. Obviously, this is an arbitrary length which should be adapted to the wearer.

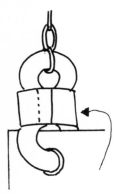

Band of glued leather

• To give a finishing touch and to avoid a certain "hardware" look, you can cover part of the "S" with a small leather square, folded over in a buckle shape and glued. This way the ends of the "S" are concealed.

However, this is not absolutely necessary.

Putting the Bag Together:

Attach the leather rectangle which carries the strips by sewing it onto the material bag.

You can also glue it on with a stainless glue.

Suggestions

This system of leather strips can further be used for belts or "hippie" style necklaces.

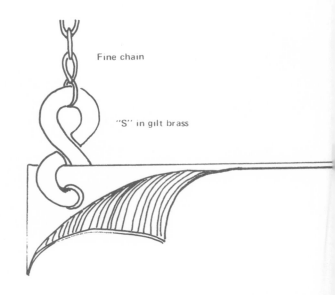

Fine chain

"S" in gilt brass

SEWING- LEATHER

Necessary equipment

- Pointed scissors, thimble
- Tape measure
- Ball-point pen or tailor's chalk
- Tracing paper
- Glossy linen thread
- Triangular shaped grooved needle
- Special glue for leather

Technical characteristics

• At what age can one begin to sew leather? As soon as a child has a basic idea about sewing and knows how to hold a needle and thread correctly (at about 10 years of age).

Sewing leather is no more difficult than ordinary sewing, provided you have a triangular grooved needle, which should be very pointed and sharp (which is therefore dangerous for very small children).

Why is glue needed? Because leather does not require hemming in the way that material is hemmed: leather does not fray automatically at the edges. To hold together two pieces of material one sews a seam or folds back the edges. To hold two pieces of leather together you may sew them, but you can also glue them and turn back the edges of the "seams" with glue.

Only glassy linen thread can be used when sewing leather. (For embroidery the strength of the thread does not count and one can choose any type of thread of wool.) Thi thread is extremely tough and resistant. It should be selected according to the shade of the leather one is working on.

COWBOY'S BOLERO

The model photographed on page 37 is suitable for children as well as adults. Time required: 4 hours.

Special equipment

The same as mentioned at the beginning of the chapter*.

• 10 small eyelets with the corresponding sized pincers to fix them into place.

• Several fairly large leather remnants (see drawing on page 54).

• A left-over strip of leather long enough to make the laces (39 1/2" x 2").

• A thick piece of material (felt, imitation felt, blanketing, "camel hair"), the same size as the piece of leather.

Specifications

The only problem is to find leather remnants of the right dimensions. With "remnants" the bolero is very inexpensive, but if one buys a whole goatskin or sheepskin (tanned) the cost is somewhat higher.

Method

Cut:

• Make a paper pattern (as you would for any dress pattern for cloth).

• Trace the pattern on the leather (on the reverse side) with the ball-point pen, and cut.

• Width of seam 1/4" on the sides and shoulders. No seams needed around the neck, the wrists, or the waist/hip level.

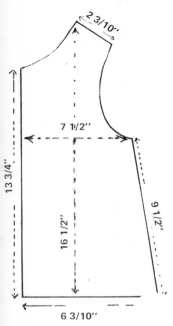

1/2 front

2 3/10"

7 1/2"

13 3/4"

16 1/2"

9 1/2"

6 3/10"

Seams:

Only 4 seams are necessary: 2 on the sides and 2 on the shoulders. Simple back-stitching on the reverse side of the pieces.

If you prefer visible stitching, over-lap the edges 1/2" and back-stitch. If you do not have pieces of leather that are high enough, you can use equal even-sized pieces joined by either stitching or gluing (following for example the color lines marked on the pattern). The effect is certainly less attractive but nevertheless perfectly acceptable... provided that the "cut" is symmetrical on both sides and even on the back as well.

Lining:

Please note that lining is optional. If you do wish to have a lining — which makes the article warmer — it must have the same pro-

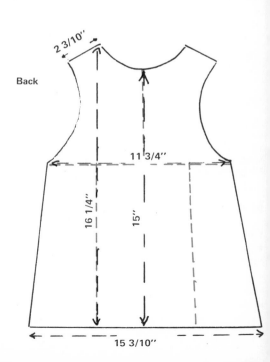

Back

2 3/10"

11 3/4"

16 1/4"

15"

15 3/10"

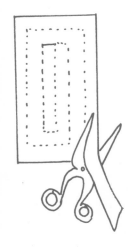

portions and be of the same size as the bolero, within more or less 1/8": at the arm-holes, neck and edge of the fringes, cut out 3/16" around the pattern.

Glue the entire surface with a good leather glue.

It is important to chose a thick material for the lining (so that the glue marks are invisible) and preferably one that doesn't fray.

Fringes:

Cut the strips 1/8" wide and about 1 1/8" deep.

Eyelets:

Place them face to face on the two front edges, 5 on each side.

Lacing:

This is cut out of a leather remnant in a turning movement (see sketch). The lacing should be fairly narrow to allow it to thread through the eyelets (1/8" in diameter) and pretty long (39 1/2").

Thread through and make a knot at each end.

Suggestions

Begin by making simple clothes: a skirt for a little girl, a sleeveless jacket for an adult...

You can make more complicated styles of clothing; the main thing is to have a good pattern and big pieces of leather or suede.

DIAMOND SHAPED CUSHION

See photo on page 39. Time required: 8 hours.

Special equipment

See list at the beginning of the chapter *.
- 4 different colored leather remnants.
- Kapok or other stuffing material.

Method

• With a ruler, draw on paper a diamond shape measuring 3'' on the sides and 5 1/8'' and 3 1/2'' from point to point-both lengthwise and across the width (1) which will be used as a pattern. Cut out.

• Select faultless leather remnants (at least on one side!) and place them on the paper diamonds. Mark on the correct place the outline which will then be cut with scissors. (Be sure to do this on the reverse side).

• Cut as follows: 7 whole diamonds, 2 half-diamonds lengthwise, 7 half-diamonds width-wise, **2 quarters-of-a diamond (see drawing on page 59).**

• Assemble the diamond shapes on a table. Keep a certain pattern, i.e. an alternating rythm of dark and light shades of the leather and suede.

• When all the pieces of suede (including the half-diamonds for the edges of the cushion and the quarters for the angles) have been laid out, turn them over on the table and put them together with pins. This is a useful precaution because making a mistake in assembling them is a frequent occurence; **always put the "top side" one beside the other and sew on the "reverse" as one would in normal sewing (see drawing).**

• Join the diamonds at 1/8'' of an inch from the edges. Sewing is possible because leather does not fray at the edges. Select linen threads to match the pieces of leather.

• Once all these diamonds have been sewn together (including the half-diamonds and the diamond quarters), measure with a ruler the borders of the resulting rectangle (here 13 1/2'' x 9'').

---

1) These dimensions have been chosen so as to enable you to use the maximum amount of easily obtainable leather remnants. One rarely has the chance to find large remnants, and therefore to make large diamonds. On the other hand, cutting smaller diamonds makes a considerable amount of extra sewing necessary by increasing the number of dia-monds for the same surface.

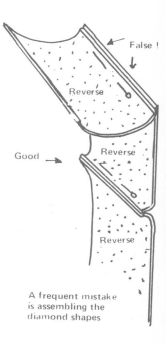

False !

Reverse

Good →   Reverse

Reverse

A frequent mistake is assembling the diamond shapes

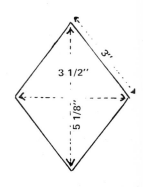

3 1/2''

5 1/8''

3''

• From another piece of leather cut out strips of leather of the same length and about 3/4" wide, as well as 3/4" at each end for the corners (see drawing). Sew these strips around the rectangle so as to have a better finish. (Don't forget to sew the angles diagonally.)

• Place the work flat out and measure it: this is just about the final dimension of the cushion.

The other side of the cushion can be either identical: Leather diamonds if you are feeling brave enough!

Or else you can use a single piece of leather of the correct size and same color;

Or a piece of material in a matching shade.

• Assemble the whole as you would an ordinary cushion. If the under side is in leather or a heavy material, you can sew a visible seam

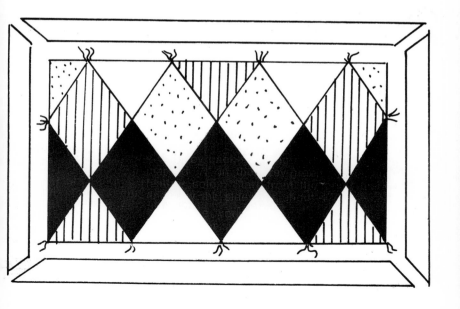

on the exterior, saddle-stitching for example (which is also the easiest).

• Before sewing the last seam (in general, the width), stuff the cushion with Kapok or any other normal stuffing.

Suggestions

You can also make bags, "poufs" and even cover seats with this diamond pattern.

ABSTRACT PICTURE BAG

See photo on page 42. Time required: 2 days.

Special equipment

See list at the beginning of the chapter *

• Several large brown suede remnants measuring at least 8 3/4" x 9 1/10" wide and very deep.

• Several small suede remnants in matching tones (here violet, various shades of brown, chestnut, beige, orange, rust, red, pink).

• A reel of brown glossy kid-skin lacing (measuring 62 1/2" in length and 1/10" in width).

Method

The Abstract Pictures:

It measures 9 1/10" wide and 13 1/2" long. It consists of small suede remnants which are back-stitched together.

• Spread the remnants flat on a table according to their color tones: starting with the darker colors (underneath) working up to the warmer and brighter colors. Study each piece carefully and make sure that its color and size are suitable to the neighobring ones.

• Sew these pieces together two by two having tacked them first. Don't forget that thread is sometimes visible, and therefore choose a darker thread for the 2 darker pieces and light colored thread for the 2 light colored pieces.

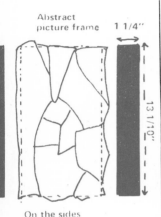

Abstract
picture frame   1 1/4"

13 1/2"

On the sides
sew the 2 strips
of brown suede

• With pieces that are uneven the rectangle will be imperfect. Therefore, when the sewing is finished, even off the whole with the aid of a ruler and don't hesitate to trim the edges — even the seams. (This doesn't matter as they are glued afterwards.)

Lining the Abstract Picture:

Very simple. Take a large piece of suede and glue them carefully onto the back of the abstract picture. It doesn't matter if these pieces are uneven.

Framing the Abstract Picture:

Cut out of the brown suede two bands measuring 13 1/2" x 1 1/8". Sew them onto the borders of the picture.

Second Side of the Bag (not decorated):

It has the same dimensions as the framed abstract picture, i.e. 13 1/2" x 11 1/2". Join together some large remnants of brown suede. If you happen to have one piece of the correct size, the work is easy.

Making up the bag:

• To make the bottom of the bag, join the two widths by plain over-stitching. Glue a strip of suede in the interior to reinforce it.

• Do simple Viennese lacing on the sides and over-stitch it also. For this, with a ball-point pen, mark the places for the holes at a distance of 1/4" from the edge and at about every 1/4" one from the other, and pierce the 2 sides at the same time. Don't forget to hold the sides of the bag together with the help of pins. Thread the kid-skin lace through the eye of a big needle used for sewing with wool and do a plain, fairly loose over-stitch.

The Shoulder Strap:

• Out of the same brown suede cut out a long band measuring 22" x 2 3/8". Down the middle of the inner side (to guide) draw a line with a ball-point pen and a ruler.

• Fold back the edges so as to have a band which measures 1" width. Glue the folded

The shoulder strap

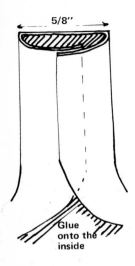

5/8"

Glue onto the inside

The outer side of the shoulder strap

Handle of the shoulder strap

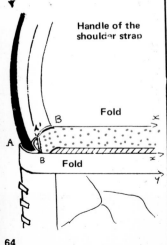

Fold

B

x

A

B

Fold

x

Y

edges and hold them for a few minutes with clothes-pins or with a weight.

● Glue the handle onto the laced seams inside of the bag. 1 1/8" or 2" deep.

Fringes:

Cut these out of a piece of brown suede measuring 11 1/2" x 4". The fringes are glued along the seam at the base of the bag.

Finish:

● To continue and give a nice finish to the abstract picture, glue a band of purple suede measuring 11 1/2" x 3/4" to the bottom of the bag.

● At the top of the bag each side will be bound with a band of brown suede measuring 11 1/2" x 1 1/2", fixed in the following way: 3/4" on the outer side of the bag, and 3/4" folded back into the inner side. At both ends of these 2 bands, make a slit 1" in length in which the shoulder strap is placed.

Draw a line 3/4" from the edge of the top of the abstract picture. Glue carefully and place the band on the line. Then glue the rest of the band on the inner side ("leather" side) and fold back.

The ends of the 2 bands should cross over the glued handle and this will reinforce it. (If you have chosen a very good glue, it should stick well.)

Suggestions

The "abstract picture" allows one to use small leather remnants in different colors. As a cushion it is very effective and also for upholstering an armchair or chair seat.

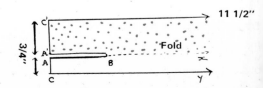

11 1/2"

C'

3/4"

A'

A

B

C

Fold

x

Y

LITTLE TURKISH SLIPPERS FOR CHILDREN

See photo on page 49. Time required: 4 hours.

Special equipment

See list at the beginning of the chapter *
- Grey-green suede remnants.
- Brown leather remnants of medium thickness and very small white leather remnants. The pattern for Turkish Slippers for children of 4-5 years old, which we describe herewith, has been made from a Moroccan model which we have copied faithfully (except for the decoration).

Method

- The pattern can be copied from the drawings given in half the normal size on page 68. There is no left and right foot, the 2 slippers will be made exactly the same.
- The only difficulty in sewing: — not to make a mistake in putting the leather together: grey-green suede is used on the "suede" side while the brown leather is used on the reverse side (the smooth shiny side for the sole on the outside of the slipper and the rough side in the inside).
- Start by back-stitching fairly tightly the point marked A on the grey-green suede and the leather sole. Start from the point marked A and sew the sides for about 4".
- Turn the work over and continue the seam on the inner side of the slipper.
- The two side seams as well as the one at the end are easy to sew (see drawing).

Decoration:

Instead of doing traditional Arab embroidery, we have just glued two designs: a heart in brown leather and a square of white leather.

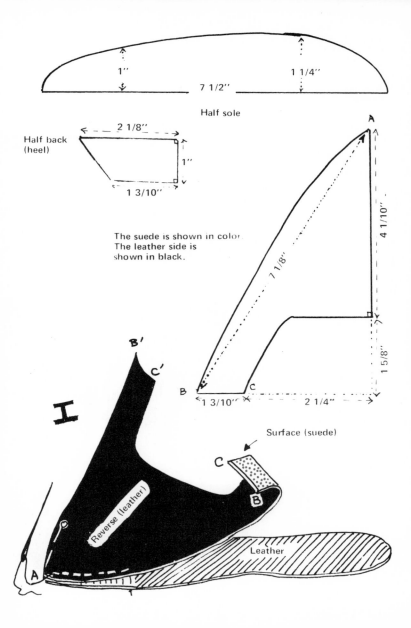

1''

1 1/4''

7 1/2''

Half sole

Half back
(heel)

2 1/8''

1''

1 3/10''

The suede is shown in color.
The leather side is
shown in black.

A

4 1/10''

7 1/8''

1 5/8''

B

C

1 3/10''

2 1/4''

Surface (suede)

B'

C'

C

B

Reverse (leather)

A

Leather

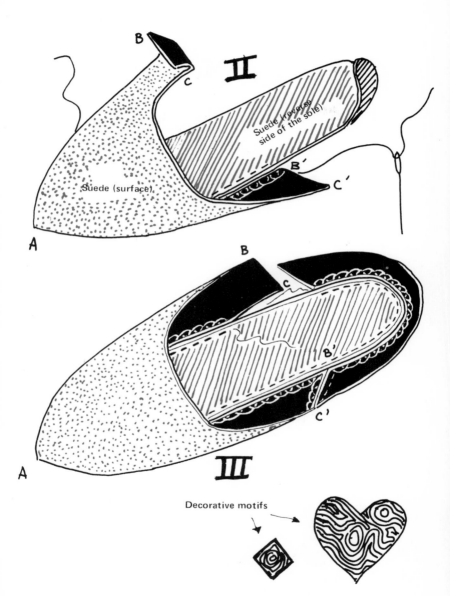

II

B

c

Suede (reverse side of the sole)

B'

C'

Suede (surface)

A

III

B

c

B'

C'

A

Decorative motifs

Suggestions

The problem in making slippers for adults is that the sole should be reinforced: a single layer of medium thick leather won't stand up to constant use by an adult. This can be remedied by sewing several pieces of leather together for the sole. The slipper will be stronger but the seams are more difficult to sew. You can also glue on a double sole on the outside (or on the inside) of the slipper. You can do repairs easily by sticking on a second leather sole.

INDIAN CUSHION

See photo on page 46. Time required: 8 days.

Special equipment

As shown at the beginning of the chapter. *
• Grey suede remnants.

• Glossy thread and embroidery silk. Choose a variety of 5 or 6 blues graded from dark to light.

• Wool: orange, golden yellow, bright pink, purple violet, pale mauve.

• Kapok or cushion stuffing.

• An old mirror either whole or broken, which one can break with a hammer into small pieces measuring about 1 1/2'' x 1 1/2''. It doesn't matter if they are very crooked. 9 small pieces are needed.

Method

The background:

• If you possess a piece of leather big enough to make one entire side of the cushion, all the better. If not then you must join several remnants to make a bigger piece; to do this, stick them together as you please. But in this case, you should hide the seams under the embroidery.

- Cut the edges carefully with a triangle so that each side is perfectly parallel to the opposite side and the corners are square.

Drawing the Motifs:

- For this a blue ball-point pen will be useful. (It can be removed from the suede if you rub it with your fingers, provided that you have not drawn too thick or crooked a line.) If you are not quite sure of your dexterity, you can use a tailors chalk.
- It is possible to work from the motif used for the cushion. (See page 75 the sketch for half the cushion, which is half its final size.)
- You can also get ideas from embroidery designs in women's magazines.
- If the background is made up of a lot of leather remnants, the drawing will probably not coincide exactly with the leather seams. In this case, do not hesitate to add flowers, leaves and stems. Indian cushions are very heavily embroidered.

Embroidery:

Three stitches are used:
- running stitch (the elementary embroidery stitch) for leaves and flowers
- chain stitch for the stalks
- buttonhole stitch around the mirrors

Setting the Mirrors:

- Cut out of the suede a shape larger than the mirror. Place the mirror on the suede and outline its shape. Cut out in the center of this piece of suede an opening smaller than the bit of mirror that will be used.
- Buttonhole stitch the inner border of this suede frame.
- Then superimpose the mirror and frame in the right order and glue: the mirror placed on the right spot (mark with a ball-point pen) on the frame in embroidered leather.

Mirror fragment
on suede flower

Center embroidery

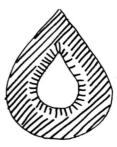

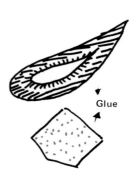

Glue

Putting the Cushion together:

- Take another piece of suede (or leather or cloth) of the same size. Join the two pieces: the outer surface and the reverse.
- Stuff with Kapok.

You can sew the two sides with a very tight buttonhole stitch, whith thick wool.

Center

STUDDING

Necessary equipment

- Gilt-headed upholstery nails (yellow lentil) with stem or claw. If plain they can be found anywhere, but if they are worked and decorated they are more difficult to come by.
- Ordinary hammer.
- Pincers, nail pincers.
- A gimlet for the hinge screws.
- A screw driver to screw on the hinges.
- Leather glue and turpentine to clean the smudges.
- Scissors, ball-point pen, ruler.

Technical characteristics

The idea is simple: cover a wooden shape with leather and decorate it with a lot of nails.

First snag: hammer the nails in straight as a great many may get bent. You then have to take them out with a screw-driver if they are buried in too deeply and pull them out with the nail pincers... then start again with another nail.

Second snag: the noise. Striking 100 times when hammering a nail into wood does not go unheard — the neighbors might get pretty annoyed...

Third snag: how not to hurt oneself... but this can be learned, just as one learns to handle a hammer...

Fourth snag: to find the right wooden shape. Please note I say "wood", a raw material which has become rare and expensive these days, and which was so easy to come by in the past. On no account use substitutes (compressed wood, plastic matter, plywood, etc.). Nails only stay fixed in a suitable thickness of wood (1/8'' to 3/8''); the thicker it is, the better the result.

Chests, boxes, different plain wooden shapes can be found in attics or in any department store... If necessary, you can have a shape made by a carpenter or make one your self. To draw designs with "nails", guiding lines must be made with a tape measure and ball-point pen, and even with tracing paper if you are afraid of making a mistake.

RUSTIC STYLE MIRROR

See photo on page 51. Time required: 2 hours.

Special equipment

As shown at the beginning of the chapter *

- Suede remnants (here "rust").
- Wooden circle 8 3/4'' in diameter.
- A round mirror 5 3/4'' in diameter.
- 8 big rustic "diamond point" nails measuring 3/4'' x 3/'' (the type used for "Louis XIII" furniture).***
- 1 hob nail.
- Approximately 35 3/4'' of braid (for furniture) or fine ultrastrong braid in a darker shade. Select the width according to the width of the wooden circle (i.e. at least 3/8''). **

Specifications

- Very easy: can be made by very inexperienced people who are clumsy with their hands.

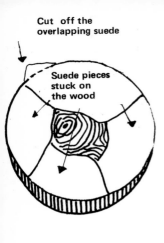

Cut off the overlapping suede

Suede pieces stuck on the wood

• The only difficulty is the wooden circle. You can either cut it out yourself with an electric saw from an old plank, or pick up the base of a small barrel at a hardware store or scrap-iron merchant. Don't forget that the wood should be thick enough to take very big nails.

Method

• Cut out of a piece of suede or leather (or several pieces joined together) a circle the same size as the wooden base (use a compass or a plate of this size). Leather or suede is not needed in the center of the circle which is under the mirror.

• Glue the leather or suede ring onto the wood.

Preparing the Mirror:

Moderately priced circular mirrors can be found at any big store. These mirrors are generally double sided: a normal mirror on one side and a magnifying mirror on the other.

• With a screwdriver or a pair of scissors, remove the metal frame which holds the mirrors in place and keep one of them.

• Place it on the leather which has been glued onto the wood and draw guiding lines with a ball-point pen. The mirror should be placed in the center of its frame.

Don't glue it immediately: It will break when you hammer in the nails!

Hammering in the Nails:

Choose where you are going to put the nails and space regularly to get the right « effect » (at an equal distance from the edge of the wood and the edge of the mirror).

• Note the places and hammer the nails the simplest way, with a hammer. This type of big solid nail does not bend. If this should happen remove the bent nail, straighten it with a pincer and hammer it in again.

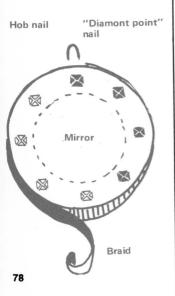

Hob nail   **"Diamont point" nail**

Mirror

Braid

Finish:

● Once the nails have been hammered in, tidy the edges of the suede with the scissors (it must not overlap the edge of the wooden support).

● Varnish the back (optional).

● Hammer a hob nail on the back tho hang the mirror up.

● Glue the braid around the thick edge of the wooden circle.

● Last of all, glue on the mirror.

Suggestions

You can make a frame for a photo, picture or portrait in the same way... If you do, glue on a piece of strong paper just slightly larger than the photo. This will "hold" it in the same way as when picture framing.

You can also use an ugly and damaged old picture frame and glue a piece of leather onto it. If the frame is made of wood, hammer on nails as well.

PIRATE'S CHEST

See photo on page 58. Time required: 4 days.

Special equipment

As shown at the beginning of the chapter.

● A wooden chest box measuring 6 3/4" x 9 3/4" x 8 3/4".

● Brown leather remnants.

● 200 brass studs of the usual size (3/8"). Expect a loss because they bend easily.

● 11 very big brass studs (3/4" in diameter) with either smooth or decorated heads **.

● A packet containing about 100 small nails 1/10" in diameter (electrical supplies).

If you can find at a hardware store other types of medium sized nails in the shape of flowers for example, buy them. The 3 types of nails mentioned here are a minimum.

• 2 brass "Coffer" handles measuring about 3 2/10" in length ***.

• 2 very simple small brass hinges with a screw to fix them into place.

• A magnetic catch to close the chest. Antique chests in this style were closed with a "rim lock" and a key. Since it is extremely difficult, if not impossible, to find one a small size we will shut it with a magnetic catch.

• A decorative brass design to put in the place of the lock ,see photo). This can be found at upholsterers, locksmiths, or antique dealers who specialize in secondhand bronzes etc.

Specifications

The concept of this chest is very simple and carrying out the work is extremely easy. The difficulties are as follows:

• Supplies: To find a wooden chest. Several solutions: Restore an old chest (with a flat or rounded lid) found at a department store or in

Top of
the chest

80

an attic — have it made up by a handyman, husband or a craftsman.

Do not have this made out of plywood or compressed woods. You must have "real" wood which can stand up perfectly to hundreds of nails.

● Hardware necessities: decorated nails as well as a pretty "rim lock" are difficult to find. On the other hand, ordinary upholstery nails are very common.

Method

● Glue the brown leather remnants onto the exterior of the chest. If possible select remnants from the same group of skins and of the same dye. Glue the pieces next to each other (avoid overlaps and wrinkles). Remove glue smudges with turpentine.

Attaching the Accessories:

If the accessories are attached first, it is easier to place the nails in the intervening spaces. We will attach:

● The handles, with nails or screws;
● The hinges with screws (So that you will

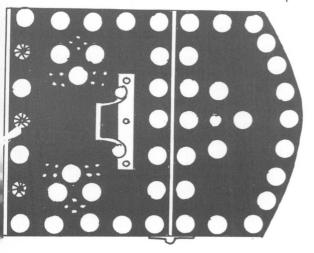

Side of
the chest

be able to handle the lid of the chest independently: do not attach them completely);

• The decorative motif in place of the lock.

Fixing the Nails:

You can take ideas from the motifs given on pages 80 and 81, or think up something more simple if you please. Pay attention to the symmetry in order to keep to the style of the work.

The Interior of the Chest:

• Fix the magnetic lock on the inside.

• Glue leather remnants either similar or dissimilar to those on the exterior. If you do not have any remnants, line it with self-sticking paper or glue on cloth.

Finish:

• Attach the last hinge screws which join the lid to the back of the chest.

• Polish the leather with wax and shine the nails and other brass ornaments.

Suggestions

This is an easy and spectacular technique which can be applied to various objects:

• Chair seats: Following a ready-made pattern, cut out the leather as you would for any upholstering material. Attach the leather onto the edges with studs.

• Old trunks. You can find old XIX century trunks lying around in a great many attics and can then convert them so that they have a certain "pirate" look about them.

• More humble objects: jewelry boxes, glove boxes, stamp boxes etc. Sometimes you can find plain wooden boxes (shoe-shine boxes or others) which can be decorated this way, provided you only use small nails.

VIENNESE
LACING

Necessary equipment

- Pencil, tape measure.
- Pointed scissors.
- A needle for threading leather strips **, a needle for wool.
- Reels of leather lacing **.
- A hammering stamp with spaced teeth **.
- Punch **.

Technical characteristics

The leather lacing is essential (see "Techniques" on page 10), but if absolutely necessary it can be replaced by a glossy cotton cord. The punch is extremely useful to pierce holes. It can be replaced by a sewing punch or by the pointed edge of a pair of scissors.

With the hammering stamp mark the places where the holes are to be pierced with the punch. You can also determine the places where the holes are to be punched by using a ball-point pen and a tape-measure. It is essential that the holes be regularly spaced.

LITTLE REMINDER NOTEBOOK

See photo on page 61. Time required: 2 hours.

Special equipment

- Small brown leather remnants.
- 2 pieces of cardboard measuring 3 1/10" x 4 1/2" and 1/8" depth.

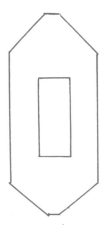

Piece A

True size

Piece B

- 1 small pad of writing paper.

- Leather lacing for Viennese lacing (shiny brown) 1/8" width.

- 1 small pad of writing paper.

- Leather lacing for Viennese lacing (shiny brown) 1/8".

- A small pencil from an old diary or address book.

- Leather glue.

Method

Preparing the different pieces:

- Carefully cut out two squares from the leather remnants, each measuring 3 1/10" x 4 1/2" to make the front and the back of the cover.

- Also cut out the pieces A and B which will be used both to secure the pencil and to close the book.

- Cut out squares of the same size from the writing paper — as many as you need to give thickness to the notebook. However, don't go beyond 1/4" (which is thick enough).

The Cover:

- On the 2 pieces of cardboard glue on evenly the 2 leather squares. Be careful not to smudge the glue.

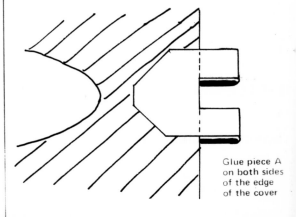

Glue piece A
on both sides
of the edge
of the cover

Glue each of the pieces of the fastener onto the cover as indicated in the drawing: the piece A (2 fasteners) on both sides of the edge of the cover and B (1 fastener) on the other edge of the cover.

Mark guiding points so as to glue the strips correctly in the middle of each edge of the cover.

Binding:

● Place the pieces of paper between the 2 parts of the cover.

● Mark out each hole where the lacing will pass. These holes must be of a similar size and regularly spaced (here 5 holes).

● Pierce the holes with the pointed blade of the scissors. Be careful, and make sure that the holes are equally well pierced through the back of the notebook.

● Thread the lacing through needle for wool and lace up the whole according to the indications on the drawing, i.e. simple button-stitching. At the first hole (the one at the beginning) make a double knot and cut off the end. At the last hole make a double knot and leave 10 1/2'' of the laces free, so as to be able to attach the pencil.

The Pencil:

Glue 3/4'' at the end of the little pencil and wind the end of the lace around it (5 times). Keep it bound tightly and let it dry.

The notebook is finished. You can add the name or initials of the person for whom it is intended in the frame made for this purpose.

Suggestions

We have also used this technique with relative ease for making several things: abstract picture bag (page 60) and sets of tooled leather holders (page 92).

This technique can be used for a lot of objects: You can thus sew bags, belts, toys, clothes, cushions, book covers etc.

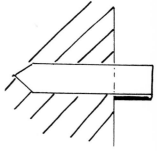

Glue piece B
on both sides of
the cover (back)

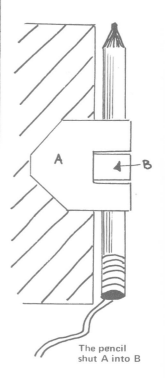

The pencil
shut A into B

85

GILDING, Poker-work, TOOLING

Necessary equipment

Gilding:
- Poker-work implement ** with a special gilding point. .
- Gold, silver or colored leaf or ribbon. **

Poker-Work:
- The same instruments with various poker-work points which are sold together.
- Enamel painting.

Tooling:
- Different shaped chisels. **
- Wooden mallet.

Technical characteristics

- They require great care.

Poker-work can be practiced at any age after 7 years, under adult guidance. (As the point is red hot, burns can be very serious.)

Enameling can also be practiced at this age if the child is in the habit of using gouache.

Tooling is carried out with "chisels" i.e. little iron shapes at the end of which are small hollow or raised designs (see sketch on page 11).

- To tool leather it should first be wet. Then place the chisel in the right place and hold it very straight. With the help of a mallet, give a sharp tap on the top end of the chisel. The design should then leave its imprint on the leather.

It is just as well to practice first on leather remnants because a certain "touch" is necessary for tooling. If the blow is too strong, the design is too deeply marked in the leather and this is unattractive. If it is too weak, the design hardly appears and it's very difficult to place the chisel in exactly the same place to have a second try.

GILDED NAPKIN RING

See photo on page 25. Time required: 2 hours.

Special equipment

• Leather or suede remnants measuring 1 1/2" x 2 1/2".

• Press stud

• Poker-working tools.

• A triangular shaped poker-work point.

Method

• So that the gilding will stand out select a smooth, shiny and dark toned leather.

• Don't worry about the precision and clean-lines of work carried out with a leather poker-working instrument (called a pyro-gilder when a gilding point can be fitted, and which also allows very fine lines).

The difficulty is the following: if the instrument is overheated, the gold melts and mixes with the leather. If it is insufficiently heated, the gold does not "take". The correct temperature is difficult to obtain; it is therefore necessary to constantly turn off the heat to allow the point to cool off.

When one has small leaves in a tissue paper bag, one can place the tissue paper between the gilding point and the gold leaf (this prevents the leather and gold from burning).

• Always place the brilliant gold surface on the exterior and the flat side face down onto the leather. It is advisable to experiment on

small leather remnants before undertaking work which requires precision.

• If you make a mistake because the gold hasn't "taken", start again by heating up the implement. If on the contrary, a smeared gold "paste" appears, rub off at once with cotton. Here we have used a fine gold point (for the lines) and a pointed triangular pyro-gilder (frieze motif on the borders).

"BERBER" STYLE PURSE

See photo on page 61. Time required: 8 hours.

Special equipment

• A large piece of pale yellow suede (12 1/2" x 1 3/4").

• A small tongue of leather the same color (1" x 2 1/2").

• For the lining, use a piece of material the same color and size as the big piece of suede.

• Poker-working implements with 3 points: triangular, 4 pronged fork, small circle.

• A big press-stud and an eyelet (optional, one can have them fixed by a shoemaker).

• Sewing materials.

Method

We have chosen a motif inspired by the Berbers of the Sahara to decorate this purse (see page 4).

• Trace or mark on the leather the principal lines of the motifs. Don't forget that when doing poker-work the leather shrinks.

• Do not over-heat. Turn off the heat from time to time to let it cool off.

• If you are nervous at the idea of holding a poker-work point in your hands for the first time... don't hesitate to experiment on leather remnants first.

The ugly side of poker-working leather: too great an irregularity in the lines when some

Poker-work points utilized

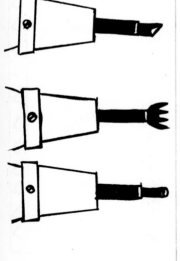

designs are thick owing to burns and others hardly visible because the point was too cold. The whole art consists of knowing when to stop before the design is burnt disastrously.

Putting the Purse Together:

• Close the pocket by back-stitching 2 seams on the sides (on the "leather" side, as the under side is "suede").

• Prepare the lining and stitch it to the interior of the purse.

• Cut the 2 ends of the suede tongue into points. Fix it onto the side which is not decorated with an eyelet. Fix the hollow part of the press-stud onto the other end of the tongue and the raised part to the side of the bag which will be decorated.

Suggestions

We have chosen the "Berber" style because we have seen a great many poker-work objects (on wood or leather) — decorated by the Berber people all around the Sahara. They are characterised by their geometrical patterns: herringbone, diamond-shaped, broken lines and regular tooth edging. For a beginner it is easier to poker-work geometrical patterns (without worrying too much about their being straight). If one wishes to pokerwork patterns based on Arabesque designs, it is more difficult to control the movement of the point. You may poker-work a great many Berber patterns on a variety of objects: cushions, big bags, belts, shoes, leather clothes, all kinds of boxes (cigarette boxes, jewelry boxes, pencil boxes), etc.

COASTER AND PLACE MATS

See photos on page 63 and 70. Time required: 1 hour for each coaster and 2 hours for the place mats.

Special equipment

• Several small enameling bottles. **

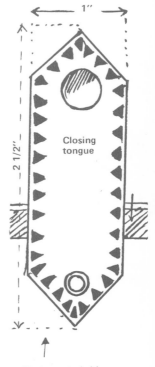

1″

2 1/2″

Closing tongue

Undecorated side

A quarter of the coaster

- Poker-work implements with the same points as those used for the preceding object.

- Pieces of untanned colorless leather, prepared for this use. We do not use remnants here but thick pieces of pre-cut leather (about 1/10") which can be found in certain specialized shops. **

- A fine gouache brush, and one thicker one.
- Turpentine or White Spirit.
- Cloths and an apron.
- Pencil, tape-measure, scissors.
- Bowls and flat surface for mixing enamels.

Method

COASTERS:

- Make up patterns from those shown in the margin and pokerwork them.

- Lay on the first coat of colored enamel. It is unnecessary to prepare the leather background which takes enamel paint very well and doesn't absorb the first coat of paint (which is thus very shiny).

We do not recommend diluting (except when the color in the bowl has thickened). Making the colors pale and more fluid causes them to smudge over the poker-work design, and then they get mixed up.

The poker-work drawn lines serve as a frame for the enamel and underline it most attractively.

- It goes without saying that one can enamel without pokerworking first. In this case, draw guide lines with a pencil.

- If you wish to have a very bright shine, wait (about 48 hours) until the first coat of enamel paint is dry and then apply a coat of colorless enamel over the whole.

PLACE MATS:

- To find a decorative motif we have used the technique of the paper napkin cut-out, as shown in the drawing below. Cut out of a piece of paper in the same dimensions as the place mat, fold it into 4 or 8 parts and make holes by cutting with the scissors.

• Unfold the paper and lay it on the leather place mat (square of 9 1/2" on each side). Be careful; the paper pattern must be correctly placed in the middle. Hold it down with a paper weight and draw the outline with a pencil.

• Poker-work the outlines following the pencilled lines.

• Fill the cut-out pattern in their hollow parts with enamel (here we have used emerald green.) Choose a fairly fine brush for the details; don't dilute the enamel.

• Wait 48 hours and with a big brush apply a coat of colorless brilliant enamel over the whole to give it a shiny look.

Suggestions

The advantage of decorating from folded paper allows one to think up various patterns which can be used in different cases: coasters, thick leather belts, bags and cushions (poker-worked only), etc.

A cut-out of a quarter of the napkin

SET OF DRINKING GLASS HOLDERS IN TOOLED LEATHER

See photo on page 72.

Special equipment

• A green glass bottle (old liquor bottle for example).

• A set of green drinking glasses, easily found in big department or dime stores (6 or 12).
Those shown in the photo measure 3 1/4" in depth and 2 1/2" in diameter.

• A piece of natural leather big enough to wrap around the glasses and the bottle.

• A wooden mallet.

• Chisel as shown on the drawing.

• Punch to make the holes.

A reel of 6 1/2" yards of brown kid strips 1/10" wide (prepared as for Viennese lacing) **.

• 70" of a wider and thicker strip (1/8" width) which can be cut out of a strip of leather.

• Pencil, tape measure.

• Bright leather lacquer.

Method

• First of all note down the dimensions of the bottle and glasses so that you can draw up a pattern of the holder. Here the bottle holder is slightly rounded towards the top, which looks more elegant. The glass holders are about half the height of the glasses.

Here too, 2 laces are provided, but it is possible to make do with only one. But be careful 1/8" must be deducted from the width of the pattern on each side to allow for the lacing.

• Before cutting the leather, cut out a paper pattern and try it on the object.

• Cut out the different leather shapes from the patterns.

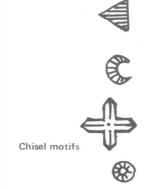

Chisel motifs

92

- Mark carefully on each leather shape the guiding lines (see the bottle motif on page 8).
- Wet the leather with a sponge (or with a paint brush) and clean water.
- Place the chisel and give a sharp blow on the handle with the wooden mallet. (To do this, work at a solid wooden table.) Work out the design using the different chisels. Wet the leather when necessary.
- When the design is finished, paint a coat of colorless lacquer with the brush to give the leather a shiny look.
- Pierce holes regularly spaced in each piece (the same dimensions as the piece of leather). Join the two pieces with plain lacing. The knot should be concealed between the leather and the bottle.
- Continue in the same way for each glass. The lacing allows one to adapt the pieces of leather to the size of the glasses. One laces more or less tightly according to the size of the glass. The glasses can be any height because the leather band only covers the lower part of the glass: the part you hold in your hand.

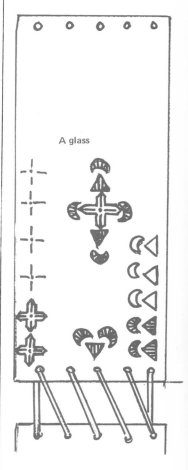

A glass

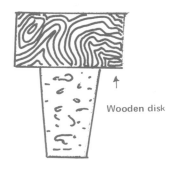

Wooden disk

Putty ball

Decorative nail

● Several ideas for the bottle-stopper:

Find a pretty glass stopper of the same color. Glue to a cork stopper a wooden disk (3/4'' high and 1 1/2'' in diameter) which can be covered in the same leather as that which surrounds the bottle. You can have this disk made by a craftsman or handyman.

Roll the top part of the cork stopper in a ball of putty. Paint it when dry. At a hardware store, buy one of those little round decorated knobs in the form of a flower, used for drawers, cupboard doors etc... and screw it into the cork.

● Knot 2 strips of brown or natural leather 35 3/4'' long around the neck of the bottle.

contents

Printed in Italy
Poligrafico G. Colombi S.p.A. - Pero (Milano)
N. F 73059